KV-177-303

DECOR

WALL DECORATIONS — ILLUSTRATIONS FROM 1910 – 1920

ARRANGED AND EDITED BY WOLFGANG HAGENEY

BELVEDERE

Edition Belvedere Co.Ltd. Rome - Milan/Italy

BELVEDERE
PAPERBACK
FASHION
TEXTILES
GRAPHIC
DESIGNS
VOLUME 3

DECOR

PUBLISHED BY
EDITION BELVEDERE CO. LTD.
ROME-MILAN (ITALY)

© COPYRIGHT 1980
BY EDITION BELVEDERE

PRINTED IN ITALY BY
STUDIO TIPOGRAFICO, ROME
PHOTOLITHOGRAPHY BY
ART COLOR OFFSET, ROME

ALL RIGHTS RESERVED
No part of this book may be reproduced or
used in any form or by any means without permission of the copyright holders.

ISBN 88-7070-004-6

EDITION BELVEDERE CO.LTD. 00196 ROME/ITALY, PIAZZALE FLAMINIO 19 - TEL. (06) 360.44.88/360.29.60

A 17447

This volume was arranged, developed and designed in the Studio & Laboratory of the Edition Belvedere in Rome/Italy.

Ceiling and walldecorations / wallpatterns
wall panelling / borders / ribbons / friezes
mirrors / festoons / staircase decorations
ornamental painted surfaces / tiles / walls

DECOR

Even before the beginning of the twenties "the decorative" achieved a special status within interior design. Considerable effort was devoted to interior planning, indeed, decor had come to play a significant role in a new self–expression. As in fashion, ornamental surface by means of its decorative should demonstrate to the observer a life–style and outlook on life. The fact that in this process form was often reduced to the formal, that ornament come to characterize an epoch, was in keeping with the spirit and nature of that earlier period. The sharply emphasized graphic–decorative formations with their strict formal uniformity lent rooms and apartments a seemingly fascinating power. The "residence" displayed a stable external structure but radiated freshness and new shine.

Murals and ceiling ornamentation, corridor decoration and ornamental painted surfaces generally dictated external appearance. Wall patterns, panelling, borders, ribbons, friezes, in addition to ornament, adorned in detail. The striking shading, particularly the pastel tones, met the new demand.

The formal interior design, the "new design", the "new decor", allowed the individual in such an environment to necessarily develop new behaviour patterns. If one observes the compositions and arrangement of motifs on the following plates in more detail, it is easy to recognize the most striking characteristics of this cultural period: on one hand the themes overflow from the repertoire of the up–until–then popular palette of subjects, on the other hand – and this has a more forceful effect – a formal and unmistakable union. Stringing together, repetition, reflection, or doubling of the portrayed objects are the rule. Floral motifs, in the same way as figurative ones, are mostly linearly or purely graphically arranged. On observation, flowers and figures hardly allow for association but portray a picture of schematic regularity. Motifs are arranged in stripes, build ribbons, form surfaces, they stiffen into objects or pale to symbols.

The so–established feeling for form of an interrupted aria, the harsh cry – doubtless the reaction against the by–gone Wilhelminian epoch – then found in purely practical terms its realization through stencilling. Decoration, related to theatre painting in its more narrow and usual sense, aimed in general at a dramatic effect. The rigid rules of the interior designer do not deny the direct influence of theatre scenery in any way. In order to bring out the illusion of space one had to understand and emphasize the advantage of linear and aerial perspectives. One had to be able to correctly anticipate the effect of light, namely lamplight, and the size of the portrayed objects such as houses, trees, flowers or figures. Their real task, it was said, was to call forth a "vivid illusion and a momentary pleasure". Rule of thumb: suggest more than state.

Decoration became fashionable. Pleasing appearance fitted in with the trend of the time. The spring cleaning of a new epoch expressed itself in the decorative. Self confidence manifested itself in decor: architecturally, ornamentally, three–dimensionally and chromatic. A comprehensive selection of stencils ensured the practical realization. This book displays a selection of them. As a document its aim is to provide an introduction to motifs which have led to application.

Già prima dell'inizio degli anni Venti, il "decorativo" nell'architettura interna era un elemento cui spettava una importanza del tutto particolare. Per l'addobbo dei locali interni sono stati impiegati mezzi considerevoli; tuttavia la decorazione era diventata una componente essenziale di una nuova autorappresentazione. Come nella moda, anche qui si dovevano rendere visibili all'osservatore con strumenti decorativi, soprattutto mediante una decorazione superficiale, lo stile di vita e l'atteggiamento nei confronti della vita stessa. Il fatto che in questa operazione la forma si sia spesso ridotta a livello del formale, che l'elemento ornamentale sia divenuto il marchio di un'epoca, corrispondeva pienamente allo spirito e alla struttura interna di quell'epoca. La strutturazione grafico–decorativa fortemente accentuata, con i suoi rigidi elementi, sistematicamente ricorrente, conferiva agli ambienti ed anche alle abitazioni una forza apparentemente agglomerante. "Abitare" e "vivere" dimostravano esternamente una struttura solida, però emanavano freschezza e nuovo splendore. Addobbi delle pareti e ornamenti dei soffitti, elementi ornamentali dell'ingresso e pittura di superfici determinavano in un primo momento l'immagine esteriore. I modelli di parete, i riempimenti di parete, i bordi, le fasce, i fregi e il complesso degli elementi ornamentali completavano la decorazione nel dettaglio. I forti effetti cromatici, soprattutto nel campo delle tonalità a pastello, sottolineavano le nuove esigenze. Questa architettura interna con forti accenti formali, il "nuovo design", il "nuovo addobbo", ha fatto sviluppare necessariamente all'individuo in un tale ambiente anche nuovi modelli

Decorazioni di soffitti e di pareti / maioliche fregi / fasce / bordi / specchi / festoni / orlature decorazioni di trombe di scala / zoccoli / orna-menti / modelli di pareti / riempimenti di pareti

di comportamento. Se si osservano più dettagliatamente le composizioni e le disposizioni dei motivi nelle illustrazioni seguenti, è possibile decifrare facilmente le caratteristiche essenziali di questa epoca culturale: da un lato l'evasione contenutistica dal repertorio della gamma tematica fino a quel momento preferita, dall'altro però – e questo è l'elemento dominante – una consonanza che non poteva essere formalmente trascurata. L'allineamento, la ripetizione, il riflesso o il raddoppio degli oggetti rappresentanti costituiscono la regola. I motivi floreali sono – così come i motivi figurativi – disposti per lo più in modo lineare o in modo puramente grafico e sistemati meno in conformità alla loro essenza naturale. I fiori e le figure difficilmente possono portare ad associazioni quando li si osserva; si ha piuttosto l'impressione di trovarsi di fronte ad una precisa regola schematica. I motivi si allineano in strisce, formano fasce, configurano superfici, si irrigidiscono formando un ornamento o impallidiscono trasformandosi in simboli.

La sensibilità formale recentemente affermata di un'era emergente, il grido acuto – senza dubbio si tratta di una reazione alla precedente epoca Guglielmina – ha trovato poi la sua realizzazione, anche dal punto di vista puramente artigianale, con la pittura a sagoma. L'addobbo, impiegato nel senso più stretto ed abituale della teatrale, tendeva nel suo complesso a realizzare effetti da palcoscenico. Le regole fisse dei pittori decorativi non negano la diretta dipendenza con le quinte. Così, per provocare illusioni locali, debbono comprendere la prospettiva lineare e aerea. Dovrebbero poter calcolare esattamente gli effetti della luce, cioè della luce delle lampadine, nonchè le dimensioni degli oggetti da rappresentare, come case, alberi, fiori o figure. Il loro compito vero e proprio, così si diceva, consisteva nel provocare una "illusione impressionante e un compiacimento momentaneo". La regola aurea era: accennare piuttosto che spiegare.

L'addobbo divenne moda. L'aspetto cortese corrispondeva alla tendenza dell'epoca. La pulizia di primavera di una nuova epoca si articolava nel decorativo. L'ovvietà si manifestava nella decorazione: dal punto di vista architettonico, ornamentale, plastico e cromatico. Per la realizzazione pratica si ricorse ad un'ampia offerta di sagome. Il presente libro ne presenta una selezione. Come documento questo testo vuole offrire la possibilità di avere un quadro generale dei motivi che sono stati impiegati.

Schon vor Beginn der 20er Jahre war das 'Dekorative' in der Raumgestaltung ein Element, dem eine ganz besondere Bedeutung zukam. Für die Dekoration von Innenräumen wurden beachtliche Mittel aufgewandt, war doch der Dekor wesentlicher Bestandteil einer neuen Selbstdarstellung geworden. Wie in der Mode solltem dem Betrachter hier vor allem durch Flächenschmuck Lebensstil und Lebensanschauung mit dekorativen Mitteln sichtbar gemacht werden. Daß sich dabei die Form oft zum Formalen reduzierte, daß sich das Ornamentale zum Stempel einer Epoche prägte, entsprach durchaus dem Geist und dem inneren Gefüge der damaligen Zeit. Die stark betont graphisch–dekorative Gestaltung mit ihren strengen formalen Gesetzmäßigkeiten verlieh Räumen oder auch Wohnungen eine scheinbar zusammenhaltende Kraft. "Wohnen" und "Leben" demonstrierten äußerlich ein festes Gefüge, strahlten sie doch Frische und neuen Glanz aus.

Wanddekorationen und Deckenschmuck, Flurausstattungen und Flächenmalerei bestimmten zunächst einmal das äußere Bild. Wandmuster, Wandfüllungen, Borden, Bänder, Friese sowie ornamentaler Zierrat schmückten im Detail. Die kräftige Farbgebung speziell im Bereich der Pastelltöne unterstrich dabei den neuen Anspruch.

Diese formal betone Raumgestaltung, das "neue Design", der "neue Dekor", ließ das Individuum in einer solchen Umgebung notwendigerweise auch neue Verhaltensmuster entwickeln.

Deckendekorationen / Wandmuster / Kacheln

Friese / Bänder / Borden / Spiegel / Gehänge

Treppenhausdekorationen / Sockel / Wände

Ornamente / Wandfüllungen / Küchenborden

Betrachtet man detaillierter die Kompositionen und Anordnungen der Motive auf den nachfolgenden Bildtafeln, lassen sich leicht die Wesensmerkmale dieser Kulturepoche herauslesen: einerseits inhaltliches Ausbrechen aus dem Repertoire der bis dahin beliebten Themenpalette, andererseits aber – und das wirkt stärker – ein formal nicht zu übersehender Gleichklang. Reihung, Wiederholung, Spiegelung oder Doppelung der dargestellten Objekte sind die Regel. Florale Motive sind ebenso wie figurative meist linienförmig oder rein graphisch angeordnet und weniger ihrem natürlichen Wesen entsprechend arrangiert. Blumen und Figuren lassen beim Betrachten kaum Assoziationen aufkommen, es entsteht eher das Bild einer schematischen Regelmäßigkeit. Motive reihen sich zu Streifen, bilden Bänder, formen Flächen, sie erstarren zum Ornament oder verblassen zu Symbolen.

Das eben entstandene Formempfinden einer aufbrechenden Ära, der grelle Schrei – ohne Zweifel Reaktion auf die vorangegangene wilhelminische Epoche – fand denn auch rein handwerklich seine Verwirklichung durch die Schablonenmalerei. Die Dekoration, im engeren und gewöhnlicheren Sinne der Theatermalerei verwandt, zielte in ihrer Gesamtheit auf bühnenhafte Effekte. Die festen Regeln der Dekorationsmaler leugnen den unmittelbaren Hang zur Kulisse erst gar nicht. So mußten sie, um örtliche Täuschungen hervorzubrigen, vorzüglich die Linear– und Luftperspektive verstehen. Sie sollten die Wirkungen des Lichts, namentlich des Lampenlichts, sowie die Größe der darzustellenden Gegenstände wie Häuser, Bäume, Blumen oder Figuren richtig berechnen können. Ihre eigentliche Aufgabe, so hieß es, bestand darin, eine "frappante Täuschung und ein momentanes Wohlgefallen" hervorzurufen. Faustregel: mehr andeuten als ausführen.

Dekoration wurde Mode. Gefälliges Aussehen entsprach dem Trend der Zeit. Der Frühjahrsputz einer neuen Epoche artikulierte sich im Dekorativen. Das Selbstverständnis manifestierte sich im Dekor: architektonisch, ornamental, plastisch, chromatisch. Für die praktische Verwirklichung sorgte ein umfassendes Angebot von Schablonen. Das vorliegende Buch zeigt davon eine Auswahl. Als Dokument will es Einblick verschaffen in Motive, die zur Anwendung geführt haben.

Ya antes de que iniciaran los años 20, lo "decorativo" era, en el diseño de ambientes, un elemento al que incumbía una significación muy particular. La decoración de interiores implicaba el empleo de recursos considerables, pues el adorno había pasado a formar parte de una nueva imagen autorepresentativa. Como en la moda, el estilo de vida y su concepción debían patentizarse a los observadores mediante expedientes decorativos superficiales. El hecho de que la forma se redujese así a lo formal, de que lo ornamental constituyese el sello distintivo de una época, correspondía cabalmente al espíritu y la estructura íntima de la misma. Una tan acentuada configuración gráficodecorativa, con sus rigurosas legitimaciones formales, confería a los espacios, e incluso a las viviendas, una coherencia aparente.

"Habitar" y "vivir" demostraban superficialmente una estructura compacta, irradiando, empero, frescura y nuevo esplendor.

Las decoraciones murales y el adorno de cielos rasos, el ornato de pisos y la pintura de superficies definían, en primer lugar, la imagen exterior. Los modelos murales, los rellenos de paredes, las orlas, fajas, frisos, los toques ornamentales, añadían el detalle galano. Al mismo tiempo, un colorido vigoroso, especialmente en la gama de los tonos al pastel, subrayaba la nueva demanda. En tal contexto, esa decoración de interiores acentuadamente formal – el "new design", el "nouveau décor" – indujo además en el individuo, forzosamente, nuevos modelos de

Decoraciones de cielos rasos y paredes
frisos / fajas / orlas / espejos / guirnaldas
decoraciones de cajas de escalera / zócalos
azulejos / paredes / muestras de paredes

conducta. Basta examinar más detalladamente las composiciones y las disposiciones de los motivos de las láminas siguientes para descubrir con más facilidad las características esenciales de esa época cultural: por un lado, en cuanto al contenido, una ruptura violenta con el repertorio de la paleta temática en boga hasta entonces; por otro – lo que más cuenta – una consonancia formal que no debe ser pasada por alto. Las reglas son la secuencia, la repetición, la reflexión, la duplicación de los objetos representados. Tanto los temas florales como los figurativos están dispuestos, en la mayoría de los casos, de manera lineal, u ordenados gráficamente con limpieza; raramente conforme a su sustancia natural. Las flores y las figuras inducen apenas asociaciones y, antes bien, se produce la imagen de una regularidad esquemática. Los motivos se hilvanan en franjas, forman fajas, componen superficies; se coagulan en el ornamento o se desvanecen en símbolos.

La sensibilidad formal que resultaba justamente de una era de ruptura, el grito estridente (sin duda alguna, reacción contra la época guillermina precedente), hallaban su realización, asimismo, de modo puramente artesanal, gracias a la pintura con plantillas. La decoración, emparentada, en el sentido más estricto y usual, con la escenografía, apuntaba globalmente al efecto teatral. Las rígidas reglas de los decoradores no negaban en forma alguna su tendencia immediata al bastidor escénico. Así, para crear ilusiones locales, tuvieron que asimilar sobre todo la perspectiva lineal y aérea. Hubieron de calcular correctamente no sólo los efectos luminosos – los de las lámparas, en particular –, sino también el tamaño de los objetos representados: casas, árboles, flores, personajes. Su verdadera misión (así se la llamaba), consistía en provocar "una ilusión sorprendente y un agrado momentáneo"; su ley férrea, en insinuar, más que concretar.

La decoración se convirtió en moda. Su aspecto complaciente correspondía al trend de la época. El atavío primaveral de una nueva era se expresaba en lo decorativo. La autoconciencia se manifestaba en el décor: arquitectónico, ornamental, plástico, cromático.

Para su ejecución práctica, se puso entonces a disposición una amplia gama de plantillas. Este libro presenta una selección de las mismas. Con carácter documental, se propone ofrecer un vistazo general a los motivos que determinaron su aplicación.

Avant même le debut des années Vingt, le "decoratif" était, dans l'architecture interne, un élément qui revêtait une importance toute particulière. On a employé, pour la décoration des locaux intérieurs, des moyens considérables; toutefois la décoration était devenue une composante essentielle d'une nouvelle auto–représentation. Comme dans la mode, il fallait, ici aussi, rendre visibles à l'observateur, avec des instruments décoratifs, surtout au moyen d'une décoration superficielle, le style de vie et l'attitude à l'égard de la vie elle–même. Le fait que, dans cette opération, la forme ait été souvent ramenée au niveau du formel, que l'élément soit devenu l'image de marque d'une époque, correspondaient pleinement à l'esprit et à la structure interne de cette époque. La structuration graphico–décorative fortement accentuée, avec ses éléments rigides, et systématiquement récurrente, conférait aux pièces, et aussi aux habitations, une force apparemment agglomérante. "Habiter" et "vivre" montraient extérieurement d'avoir une structure solide, mais ils dégageaint cependant de la fraîcheur et une splendeur nouvelle. Les décorations des parois et les ornements des plafonds, les éléments ornementaux de l'entrée et la peinture des surfaces déterminaient, en un premier moment, l'image extérieure. Les modèles de paroi, les garnissages de paroi, les bordures, les bandes, les frises et l'ensemble des divers éléments ornementaux complétaient la décoration dans le détail. Les effets chromatiques marqués, surtout dans le domaine des tons au pastel, soulignaient les nouvelles exigences.

Décorations de plafonds et murales / parois frises / bandes / glaces / festons / socles / décoration de la cage d'escalier / bordures / modèles muraux / garnissage de paroi / ornements

Cette architecture aux forts accents formels, ce "nouveau design", cette "nouvelle décoration", a eu nécessairement comme conséquence que, dans une telle ambiance, de nouveaux modèles comportement se sont manifestés chez l'individu. Si l'on observe plus en détail les compositions et les dispositions des motifs dans les illustrations qui suivent, on parvient alors à déchiffrer aisément les caractéristiques essentielles de cette époque culturelle: pour ce qui a trait aux contenus, d'une part, l'évasion du répertoire de la gamme de thèmes préférée jusqu'alors et, d'autre part cependant une consonance qui ne pouvait être formellement négligée. L'alignement, la répétition, le reflet ou le redoublement des objets représentés sont la règle. Les motifs floraux – tout comme les motifs figuratifs – disposés, pour la plupart, de façon linéaire ou purement graphique sont arrangés moins conformément à leur essence naturelle. Les motifs sont alignés en rayures, ils forment des bandes, ils représentent des surfaces, ils se figent, formant ainsi un ornement, ou bien ils pâlissent et se transforment alors en symboles.

La sensibilité formelle, qui s'est affirmée récemment, d'une ère émergente, le cri aigu – il s'agit, sans aucun doute, d'une réaction à la précédente époque Guillaume II – a trouvé ensuite sa réalisation, même du point de vue purement artisanal, avec la peinture en silhouette. La décoration, employée dans le sens plus étroit et habituel de la peinture théâtrale, tendait, dans son ensemble, à réaliser des effets scéniques. Les règles fixes des peintres décoratifs ne nient pas la dépendance étroite avec les coulisses. De sorte que, pour provoquer des illusions locales, ils doivent comprendre la perspective linéaire et aérienne. Ils devraient pouvoir calculer exactement les effets de la lumière, c'est–à–dire celle des ampoules, ainsi que les dimensions des objets à représenter, tels que les maisons, les arbres, les fleurs ou les figures. Leur tâche proprement dite, affirmait–on, consistait à provoquer une "illusion impressionnante et une satisfaction momentanée". La règle d'or était: esquisser plutôt qu'expliquer. La décoration devient mode. L'aspect courtois correspondait à la tendance de l'époque. Le nettoyage de printemps d'une nouvelle époque était constitué par le décoratif. L'évidence se manifestait dans la décoration: du point de vue architectonique, ornemental, plastique et chromatique. Pour la réalisation pratique, on a recours à une vaste offre de silhouettes. Le présent livre en fournit une sélection. En tant que document, ce texte veut offrir la possibilité d'avoir un tableau général des motifs qui ont été employés.

Contents
Explanations to the following plates

Indice
Spiegazioni delle tavole illustrative successive

Inhalt
Erklärungen zu den nachfolgenden Bildtafeln

Indice
Leyendas acerca de las ilustraciones siguientes

Sommaire

Explication des tableaux d'illustration suivants

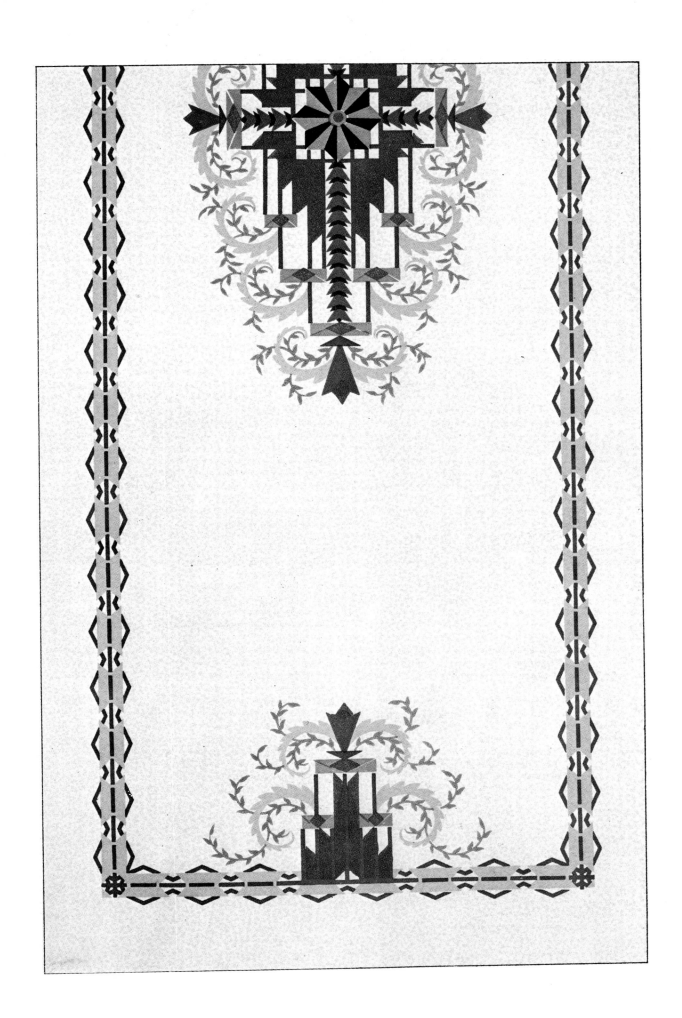

31

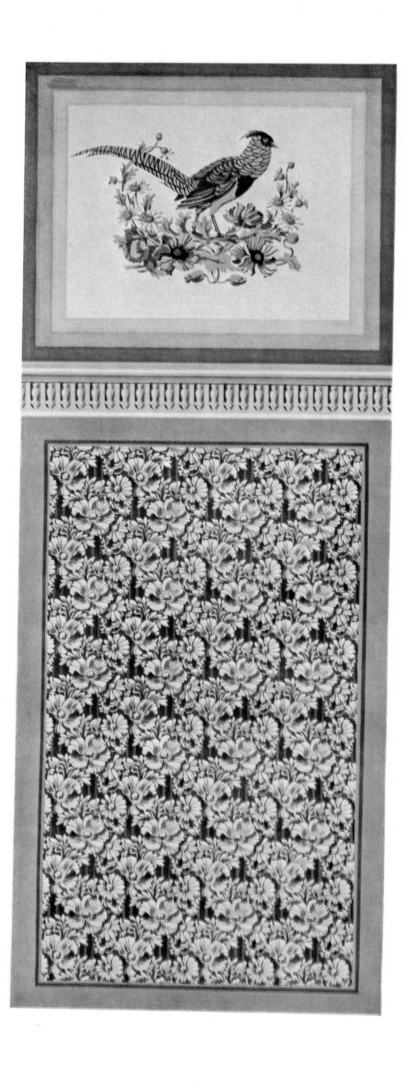

32

33

37

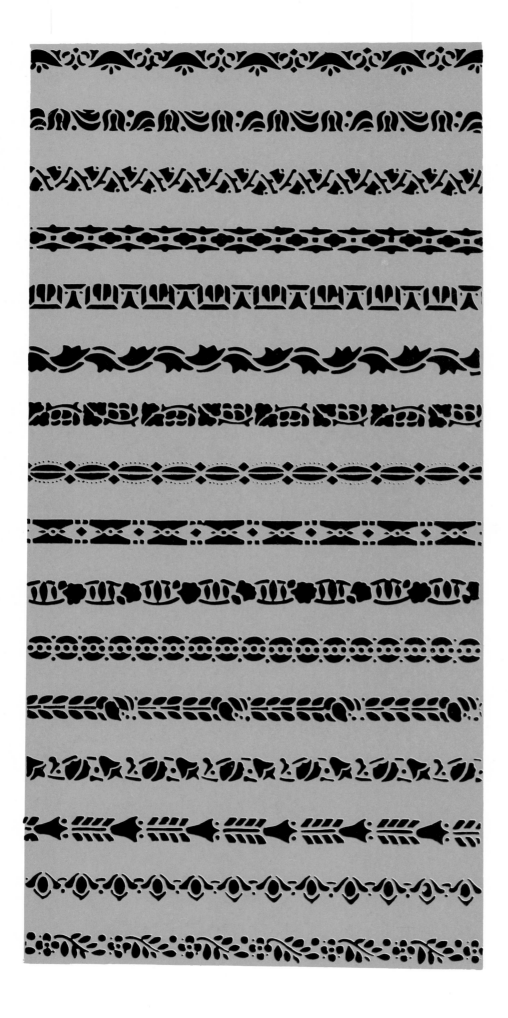
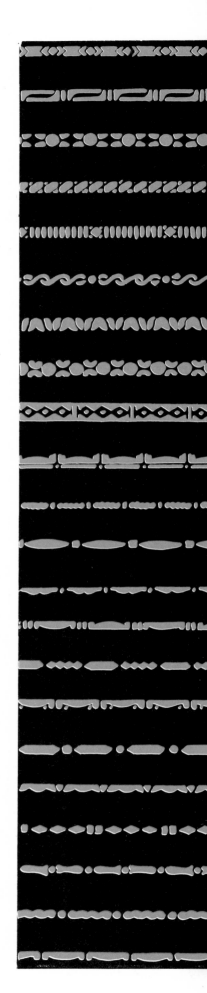

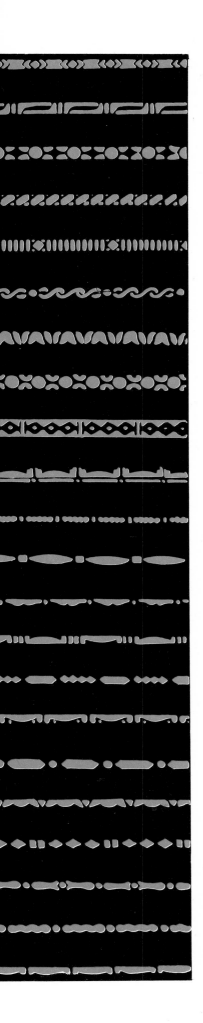
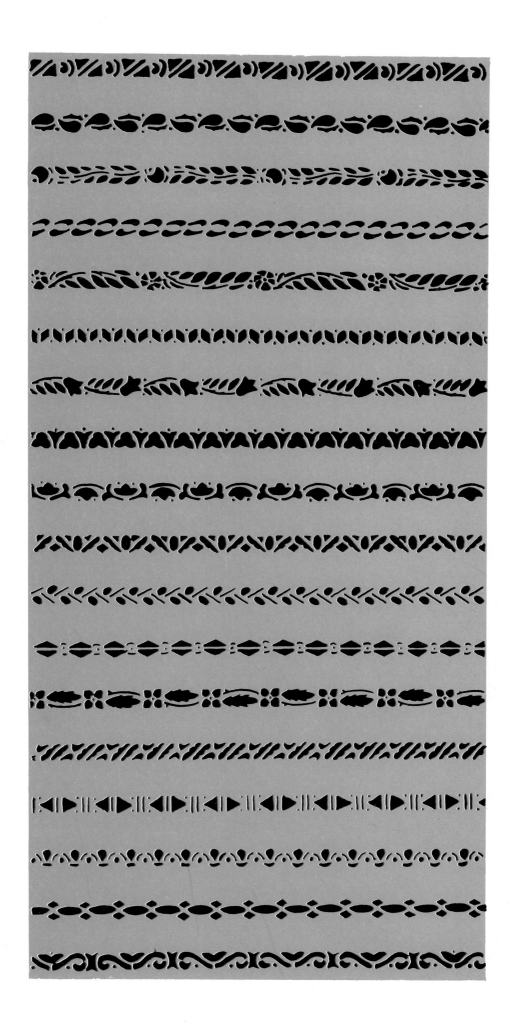

40

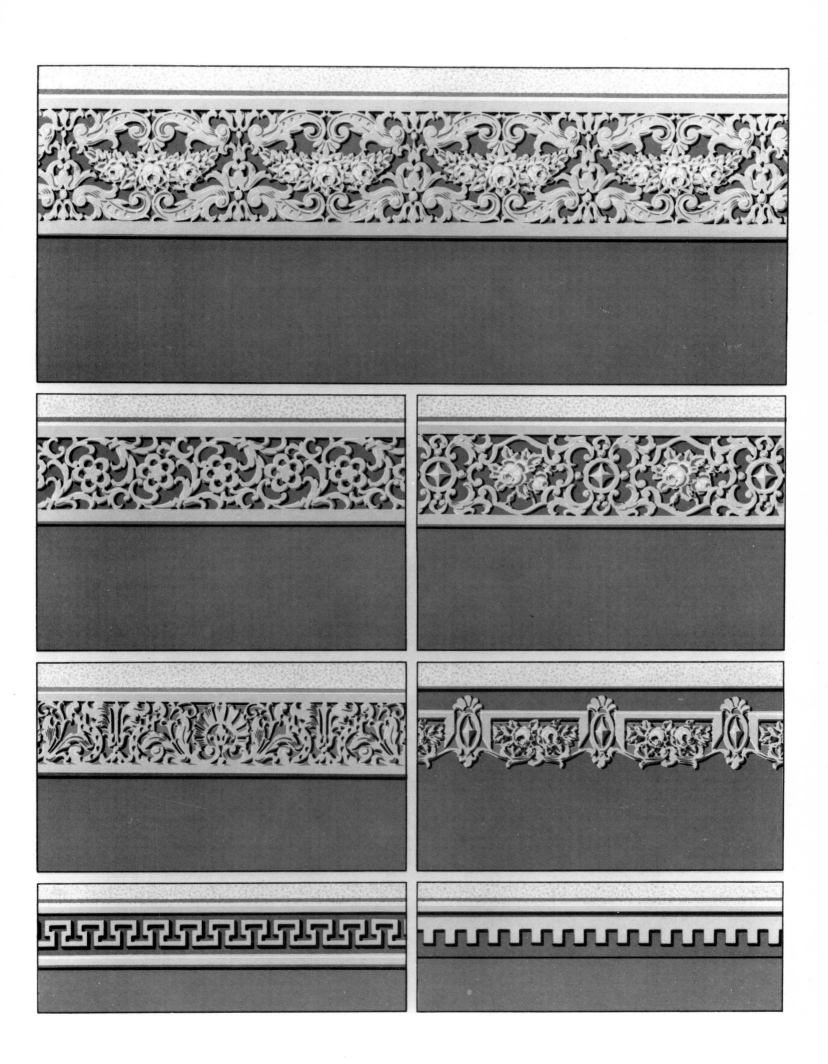

41

42

43

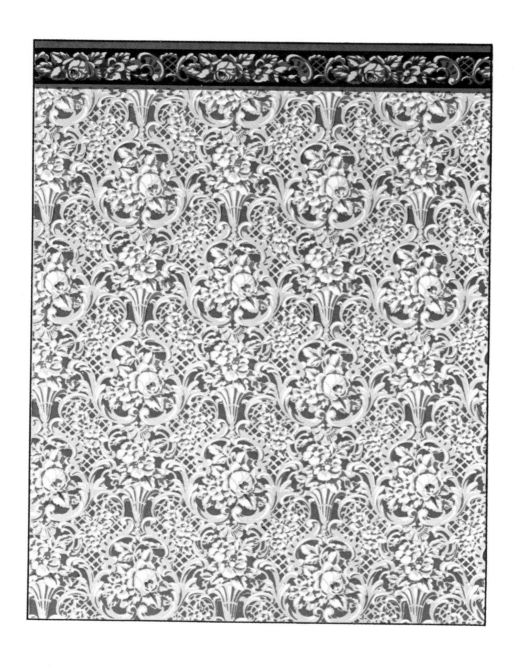

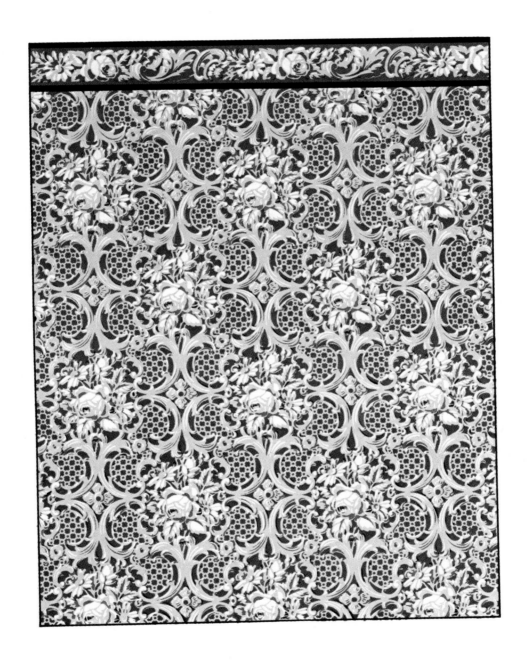

45

46

47

49

51

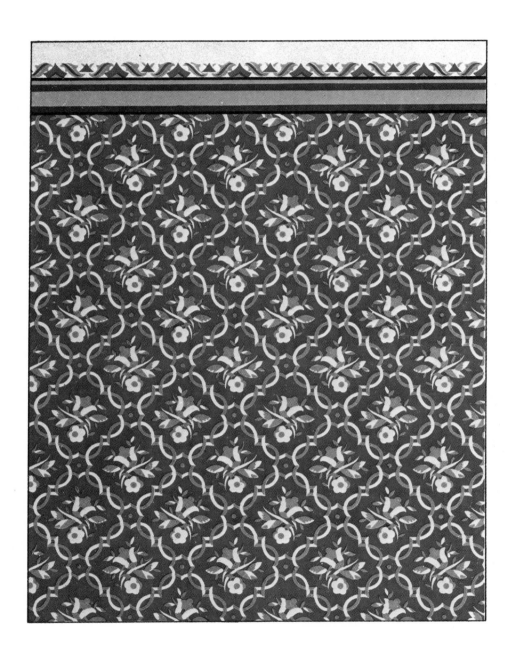

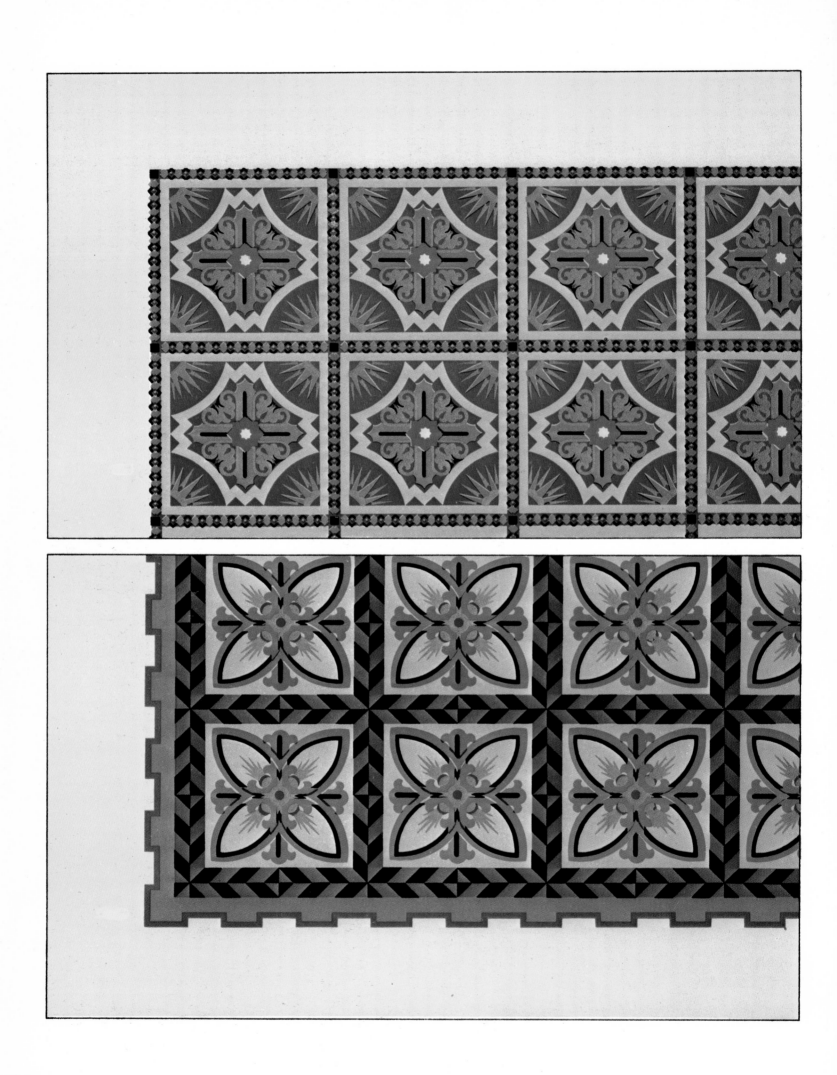

65

69

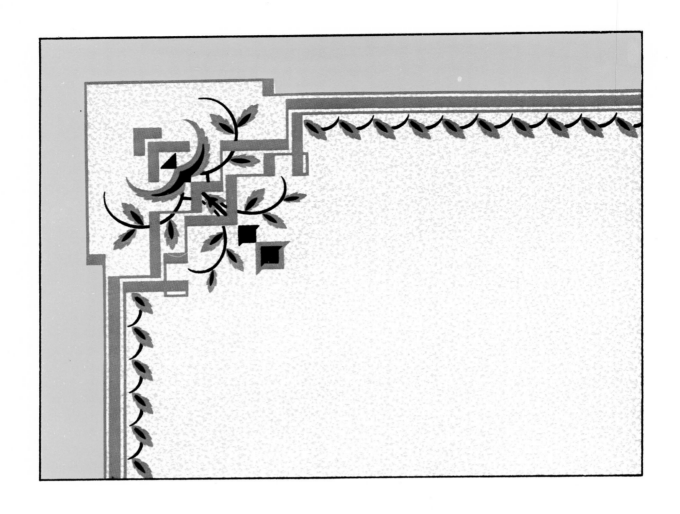

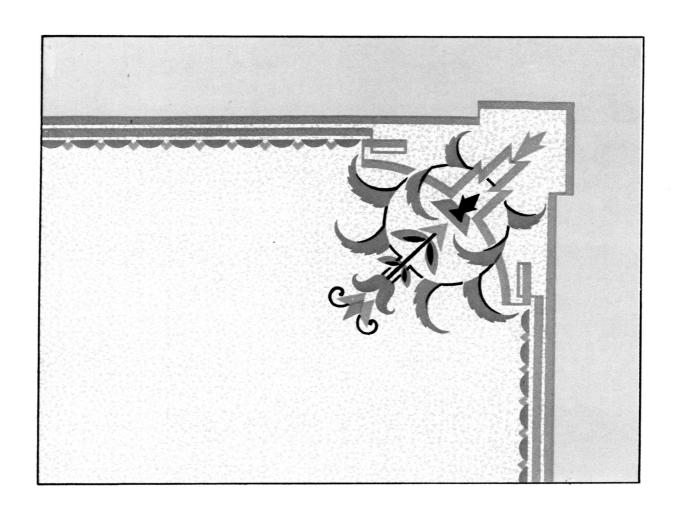

79

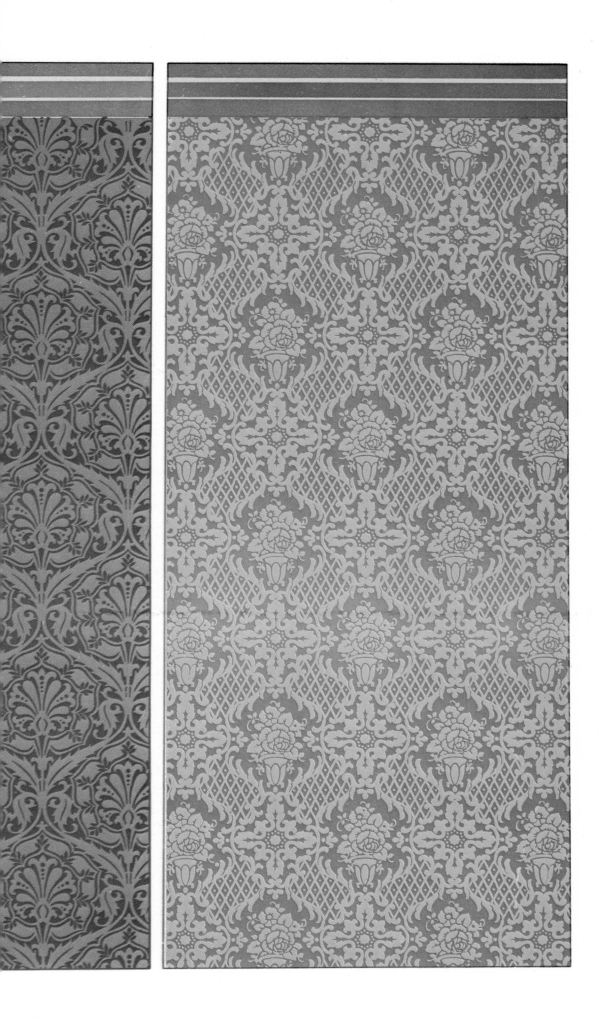

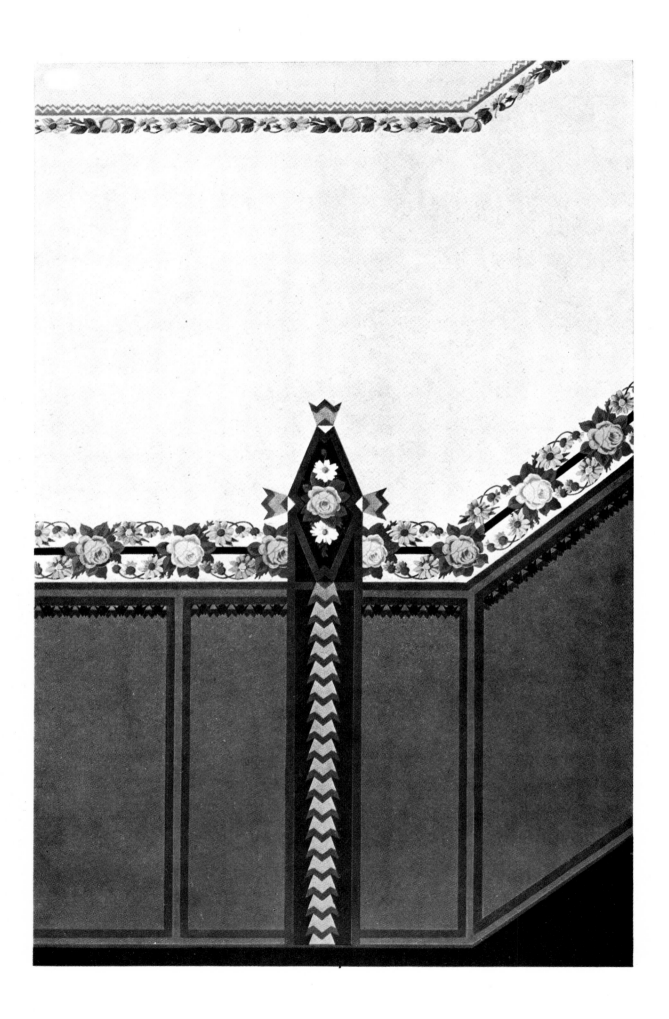

94

95

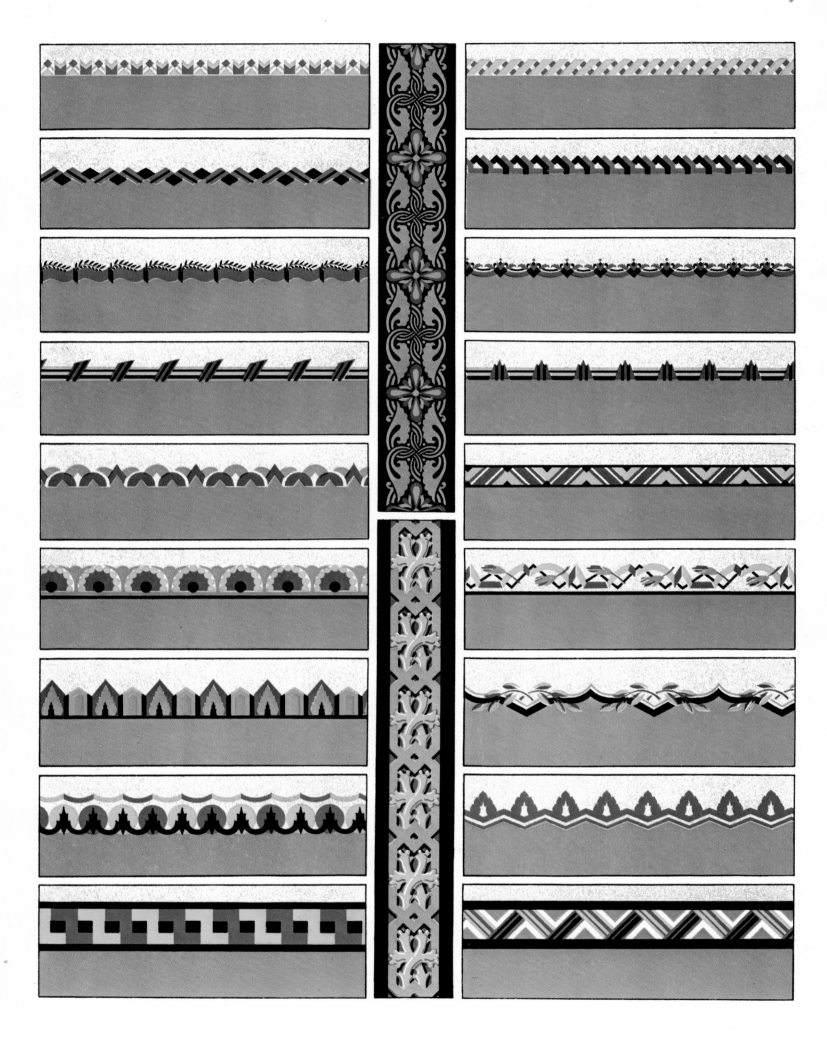

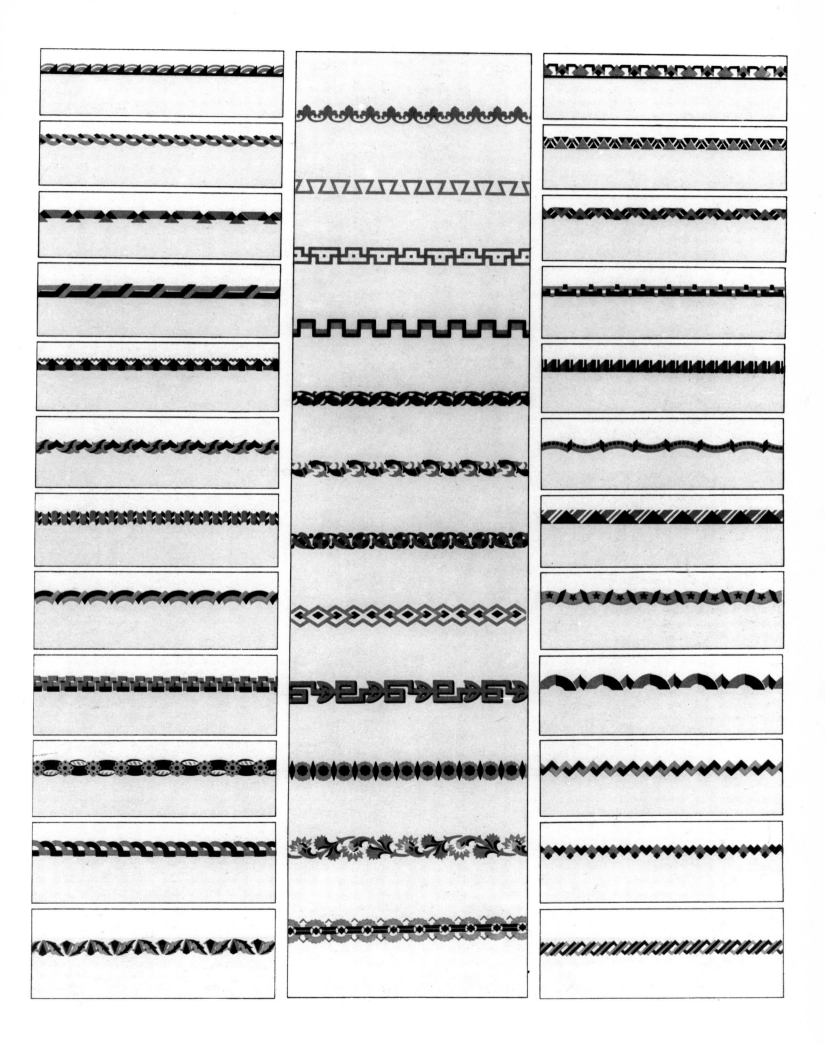

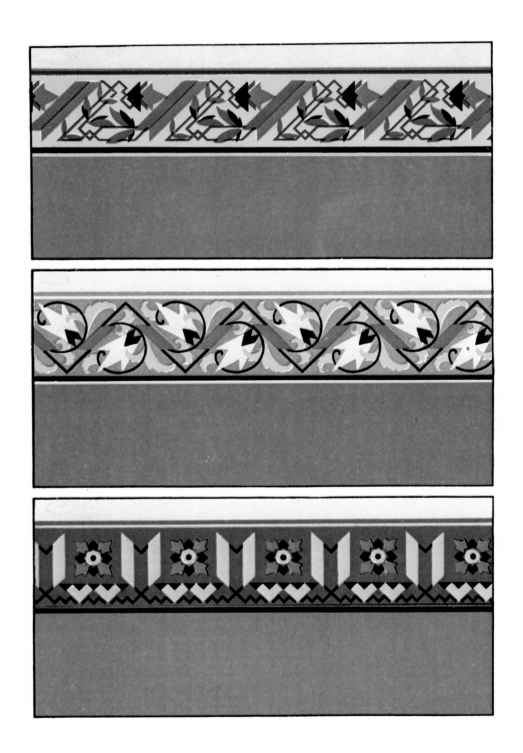

106

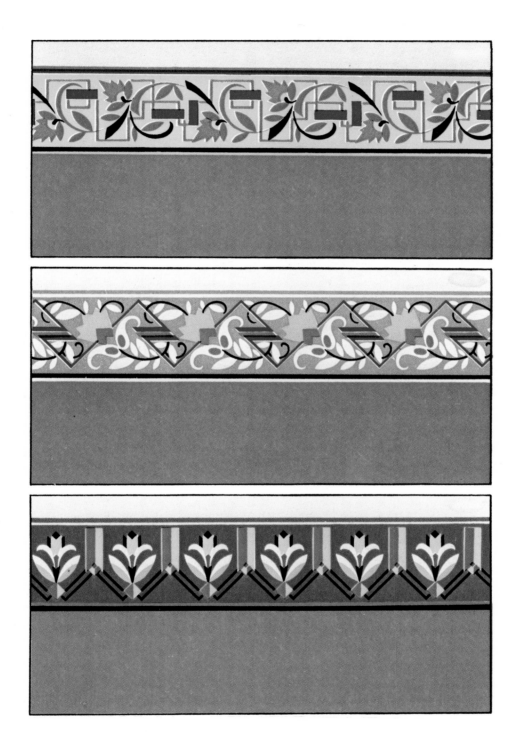

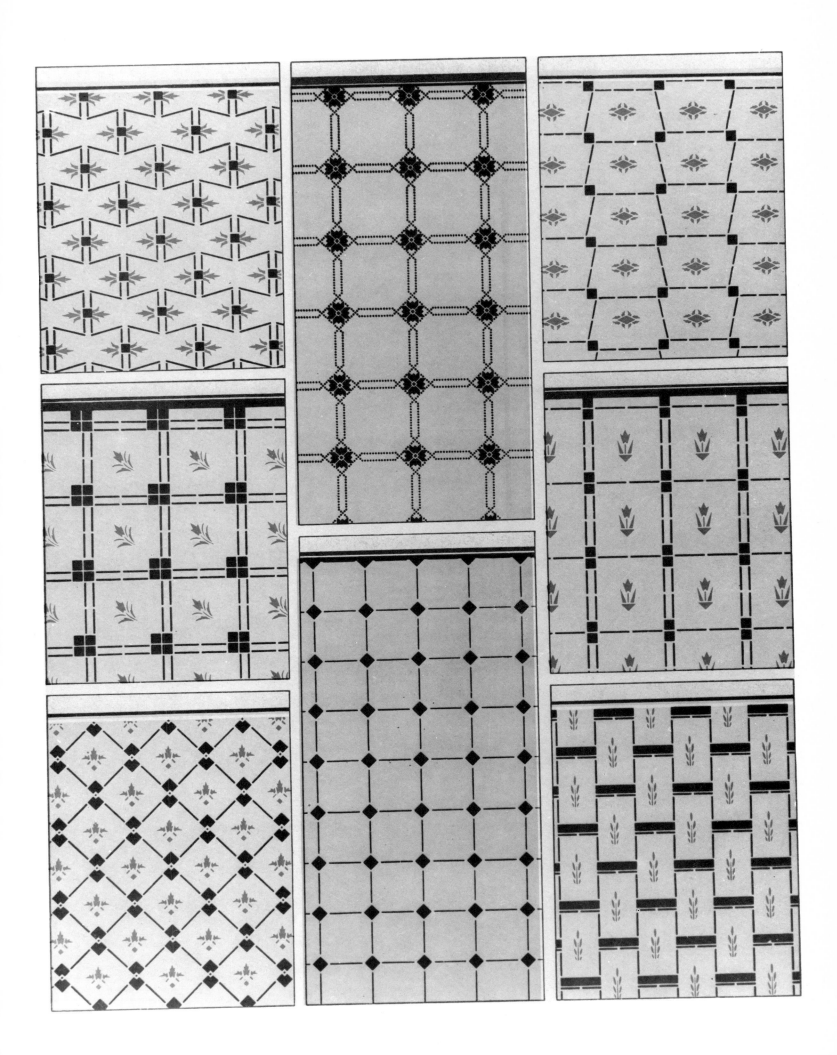

117

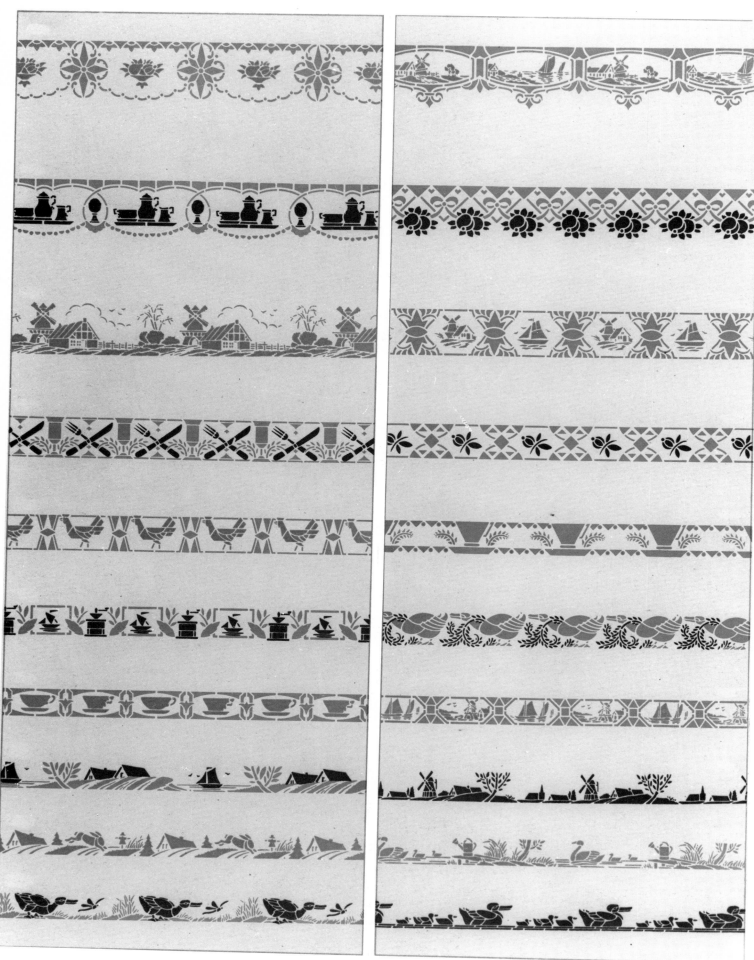

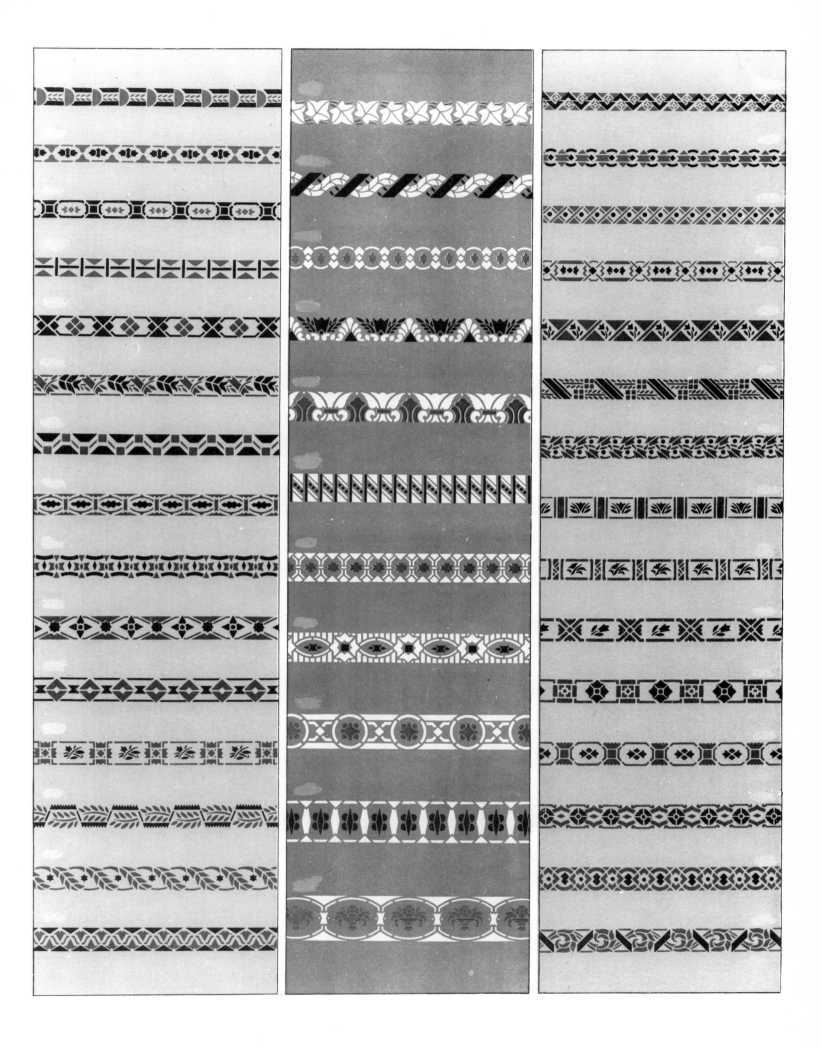

119

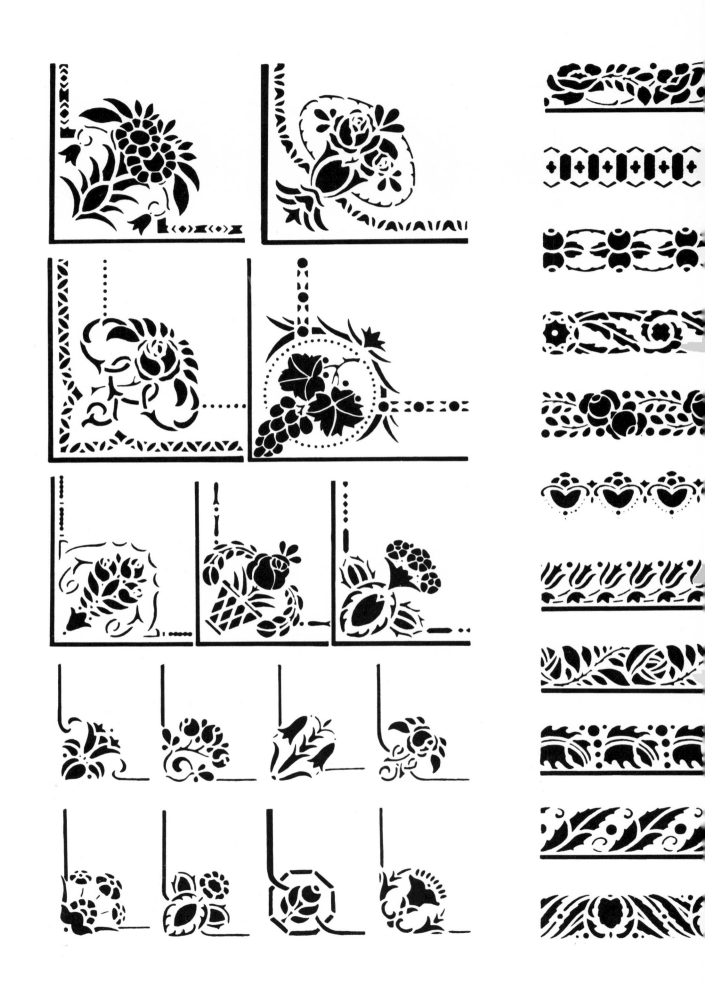

131

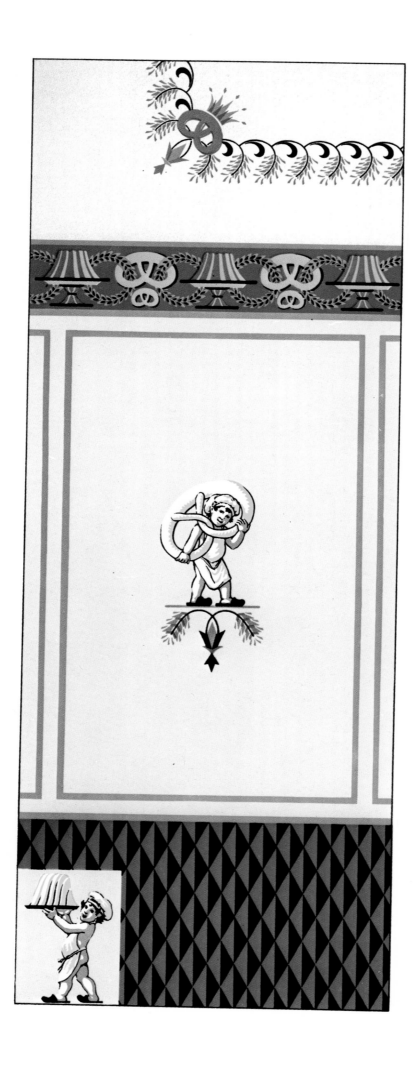

134

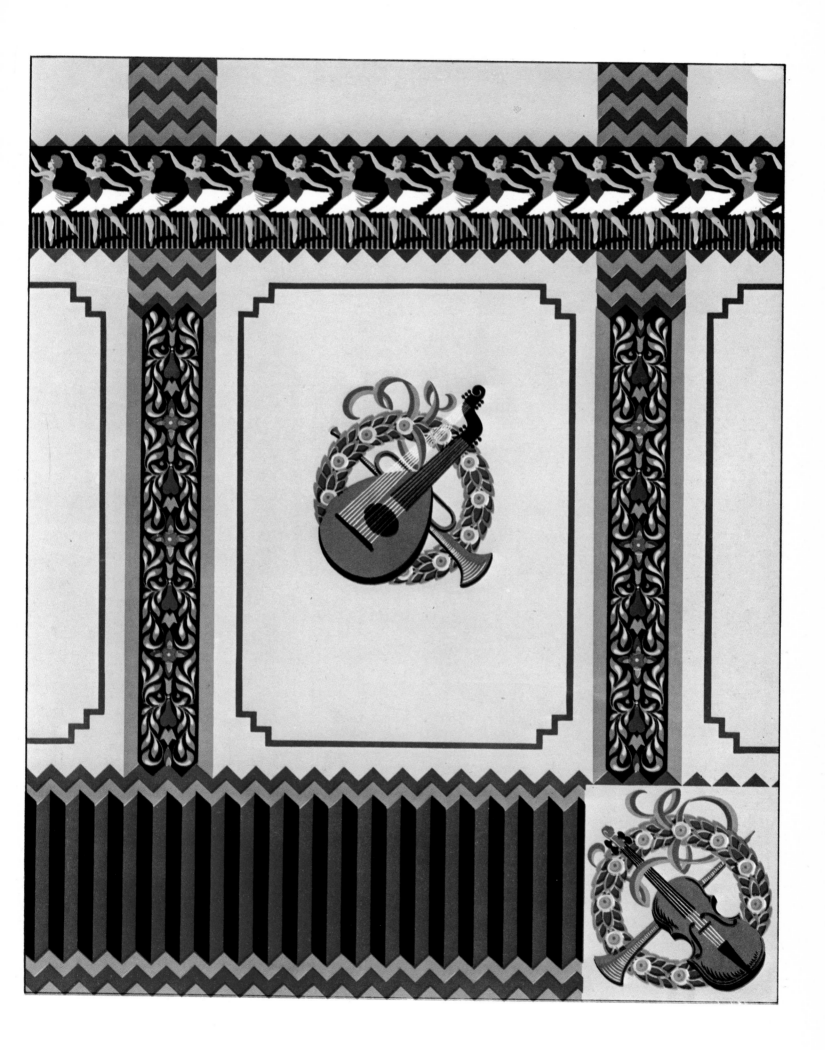

141

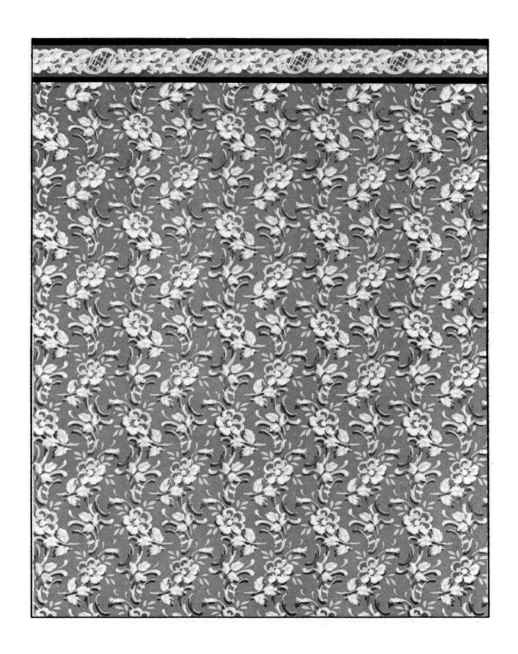

143

144

149

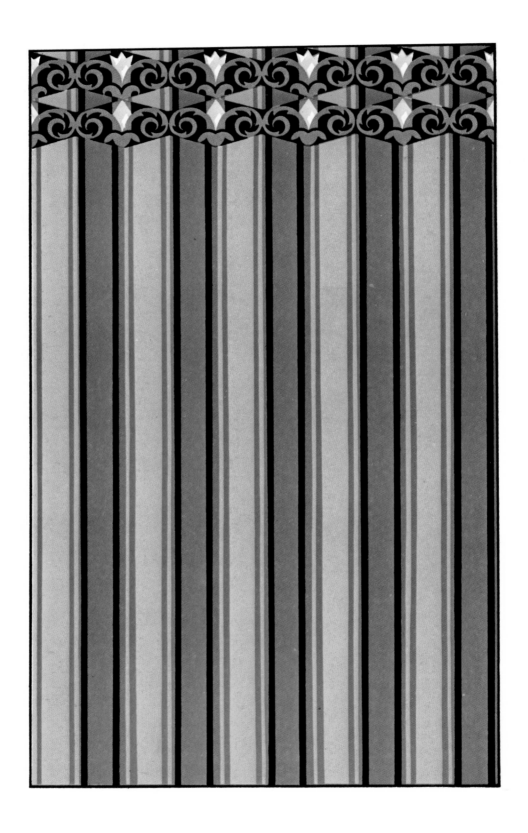

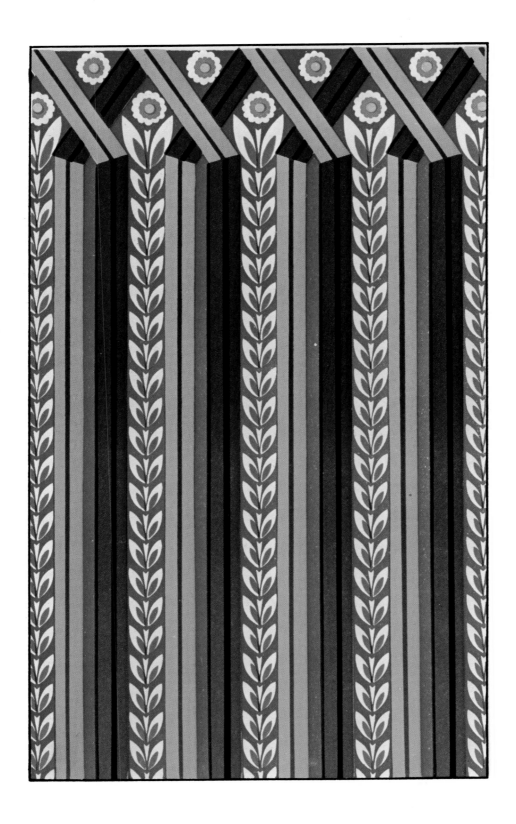

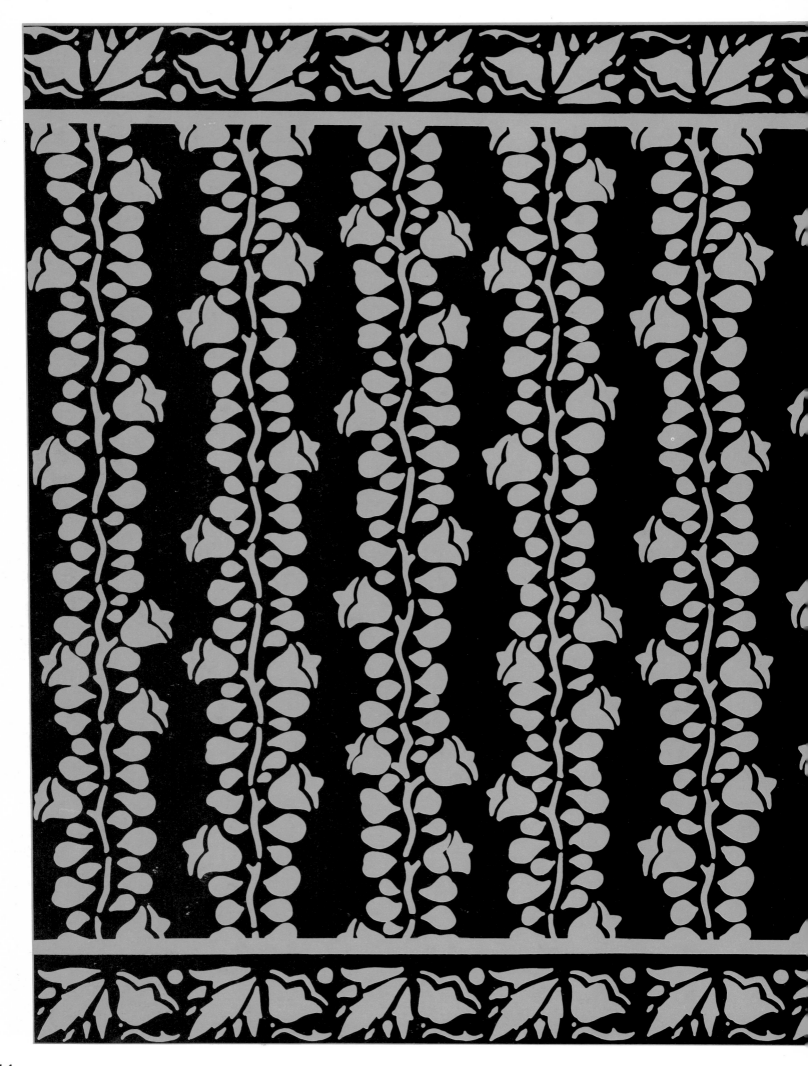

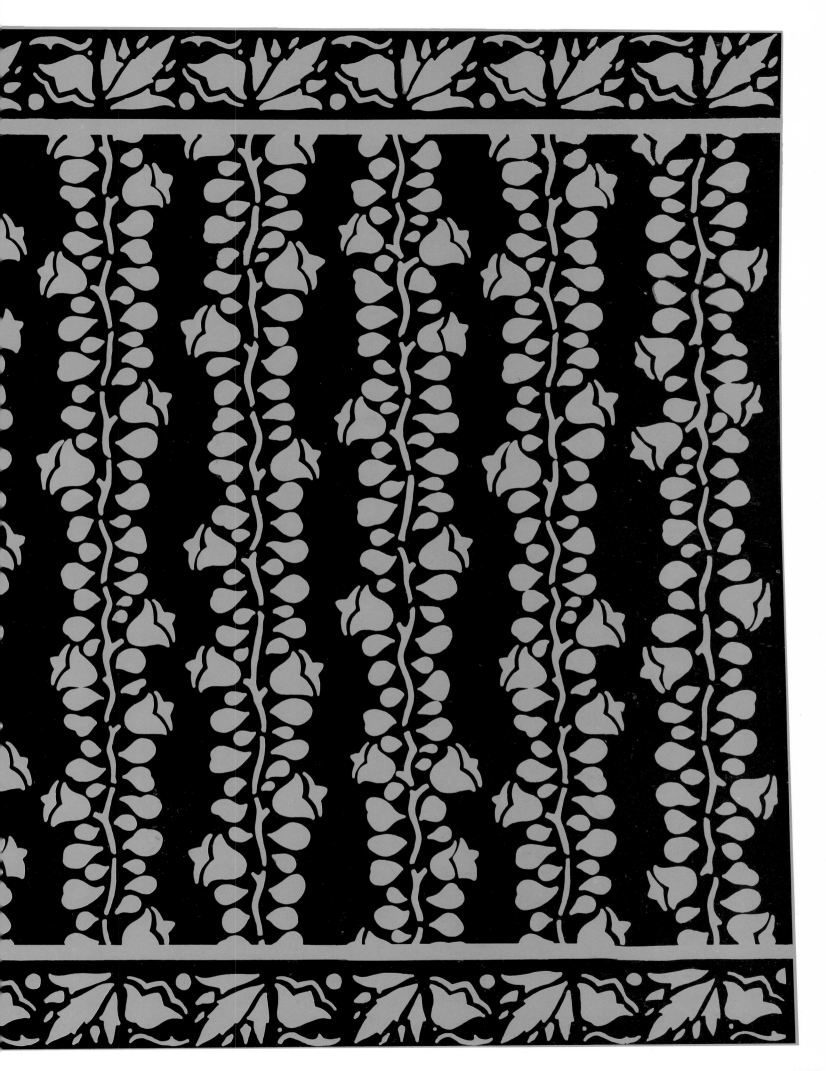

175

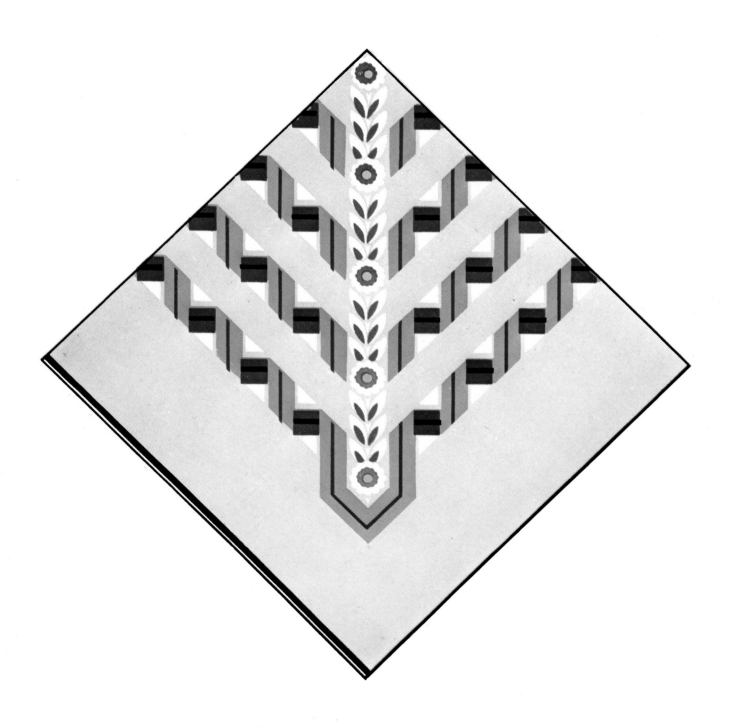

176

180

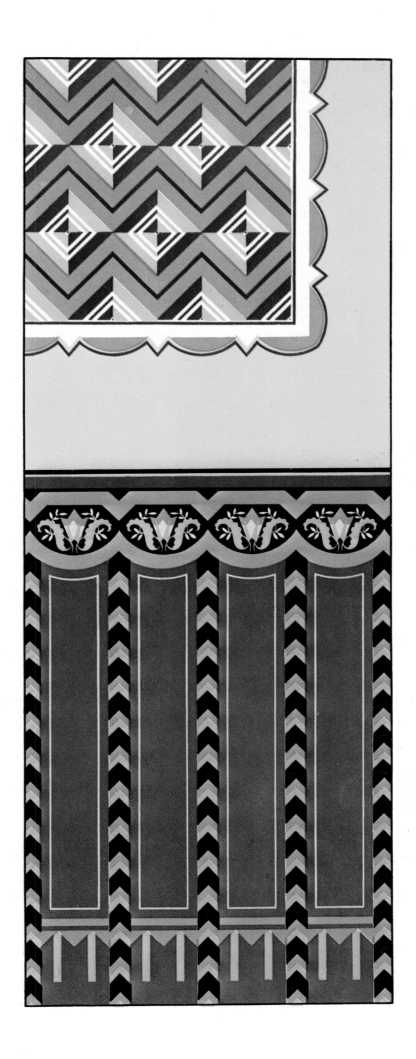

185

186

190

191

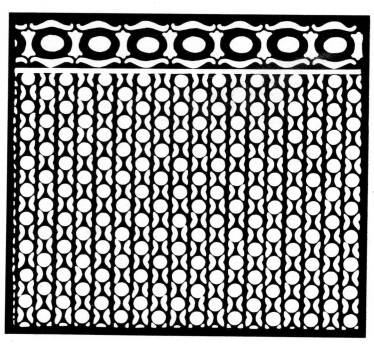

192

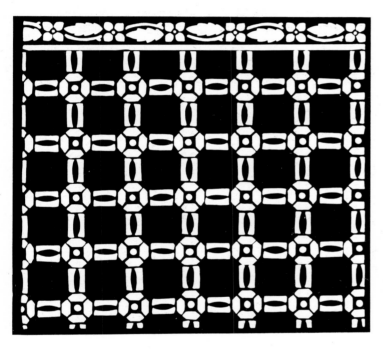

193

194

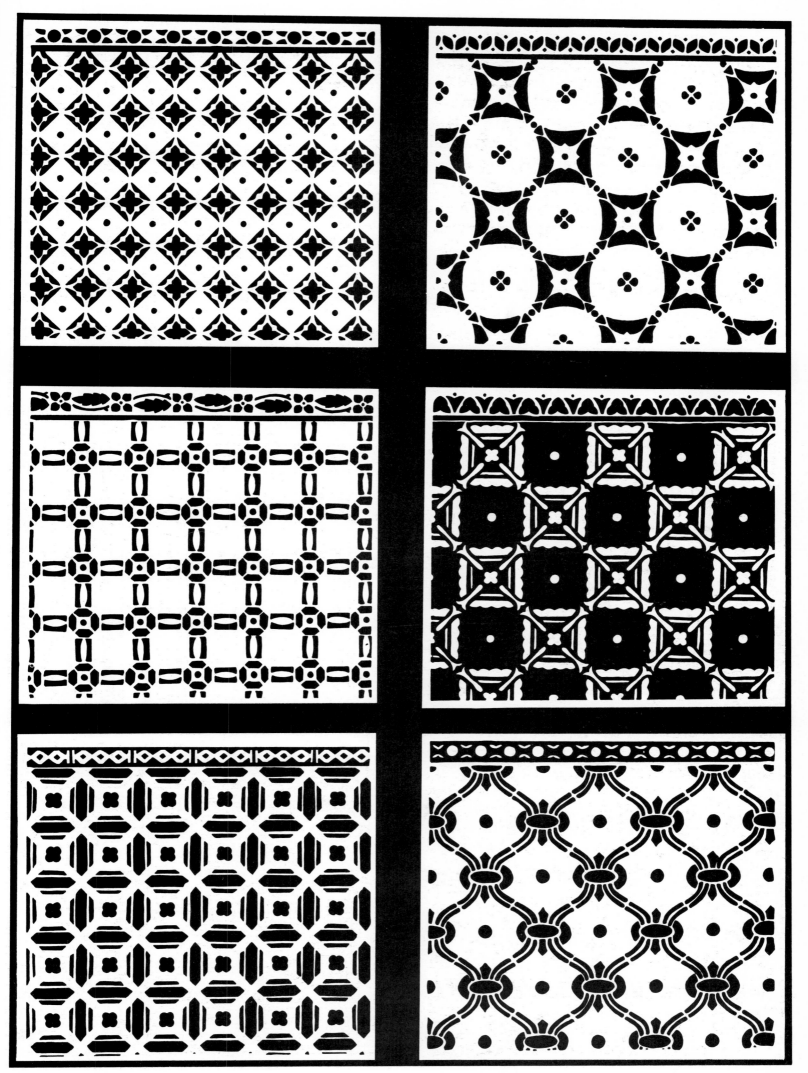

196

Also published by

BELVEDERE

Flower Composition
The Plants of 1917
Natural Flowers & Herbs
Floral Art
Flower & Ornament
Beauties of Nature
Blumen

BELVEDERE

Edition Belvedere Co.Ltd. Rome - Milan/Italy

...books for fashion, textile & graphic design ...
...ideas for wallpaper, home furnishing & interior design ...
...material for decoration, illustration & advertising...

FLORAL DREAM

120 COLOR PLATES

OF JAPANESE

FLOWER MOTIFS

BELVEDERE

BELVEDERE HARDCOVER

BELVEDERE HARDCOVER

EXAMPLES OF CHINESE ORNAMENT

100 Plates in colour selected from objects in the South Kensington Museum and other collectors

by

OWEN JONES

Examples of Chinese Ornament was first published in London 1867. Today the work is one of the most sought-after antiquarian books of the Victorian Era and art collectors consider it to be a bibliophil's rarity. This Reprint is based on an original 1867 draft.

Owen Jones, as an English architect, designer and writer was particular inspired by Islamic art. In his capacity as superintendent of works for The Great London Exhibition 1851, he created a new style of design for The Crystal Palace at Sydenham. In 1856 he first published his major work with the title *Grammar of Ornament*, the first comprehensive illustrated book about the ornaments of different peoples, cultural circles and epochs.

« We have long been familiar with the power of the Chinese to balance colours, but we were not so well acquainted with their power of treating purely ornamental or conventional forms...

...The position of the larger flowers was fixed in the position most suited to develope the peculiar form of the vase, and the whole surface was set out by these flowers into symmetrical proportional areas; here law and order were abandoned, and the instinct and caprice of the artist came into play, in uniting all these fixed centres by a flowing line. This flowing line then dividing the different triangular spaces irregularly, masses of intermediate size, either as flowers or large leaves, were put in, springing from the continuous line; these secondary masses also balance triangularly, but in a less rigid manner than with the larger flowers: the process is continued by the introduction within the intermediate spaces of still smaller forms, buds, or stalks, till the whole is filled up, and repose

is obtained by evenness of tint. This method of composition is followed in all the Oriental styles of ornament: what is peculiar to the Chinese, especially in their large enamelled objects, is the large relative size of the principal flowers which mark the triangulation of the areas; and it will be seen throughout the plates how cleverly this apparent disproportion of the principal points of the composition is got over by the detail on the surface of the flower, so that the desirable evenness of tint is preserved...

...The scheme of colouring of the Chinese is peculiarly their own. They deal principally with broken colours: pale blue, pale green, and pale pink for the masses; dark pink, dark green, purple, and yellow and white, in much smaller quantities. There is nothing crude or harsh in any of their compositions; the eye is perfectly satisfied with the balance and arrangement of both form and colour... »

Preface to *Examples
of Chinese Ornament*

EXAMPLES OF
CHINESE ORNAMENT

ISBN 88-7070-003-8

BELVEDERE - PAPERBACKS

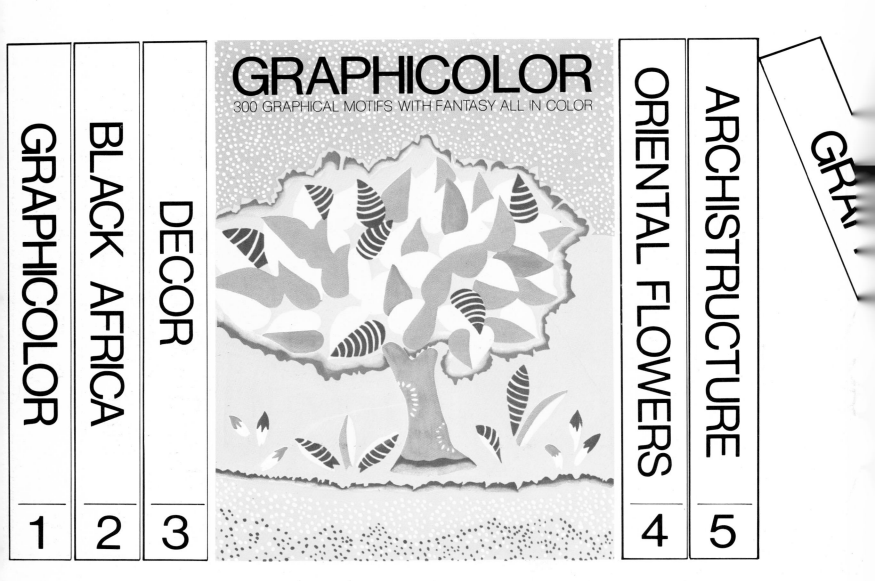

GRAPHICOLOR

BLACK AFRICA

DECOR

GRAPHICOLOR
300 GRAPHICAL MOTIFS WITH FANTASY ALL IN COLOR

ORIENTAL FLOWERS

ARCHISTRUCTURE

GRA...

1   2   3   4   5

300 imaginative graphic motifs — all in color — reproduced on 96 plates, illustrate a variety of optical-decorative inspirations whose origin is to be found in a walk of observation through nature. The experience of the moment, the intuition, the principle of play are vital and decisive — ...a drop of water falling from the gutter onto the veranda... the wind blowing a leaf from a tree onto a park bench... a flower casting its shadow onto dead leaves... — these are moments which the artist attempts to transform into design. Graphic designs come into existence. Decorative graphic from every-day-life. The world of nature becomes formalized. Everything is recorded, transformed, finds new expression in form, color, space, achieves a new dimension — becomes design.

ISBN 88-7070-001-1

BELVEDERE - PAPERBACKS

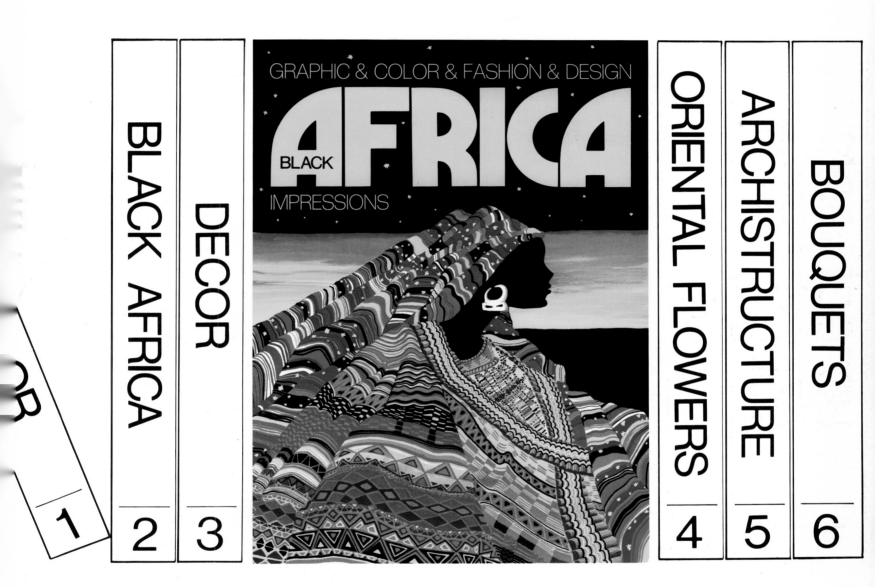

GRAPHIC & COLOR & FASHION & DESIGN

BLACK AFRICA

IMPRESSIONS

BLACK AFRICA — 2

DECOR — 3

ORIENTAL FLOWERS — 4

ARCHISTRUCTURE — 5

BOUQUETS — 6

— 1

Isn't African culture a fascinating mine of resources just as much now in the present as it has been in the past? And hasn't modern art profitted from this fact up until now? Afro-culture is vitally alive. Africa, with its ''primitive art'' still possesses an immeasurable potential: originality, spontaneity, instict, imagination and self-confidence. This book shows African folklore transformed into graphic design, where nature, light, color, lifestyle, environment, clothing and jewellery are symbolically representend. The result is a free graphic interpretation of the African form of expression and creation. BLACK AFRICA is an ornamental/ decorative style of art — a travel guide for the senses.

ISBN 88-7070-002-X

BELVEDERE BOOK BOXES

FLOWER COMPOSITION

Based upon dress fabrics of 1940 - 100 different floral motifs with 400 suggested exemplary variations are printed on both sides of 150 single plates, with positive-negative-effects, reductions and blow-ups.
Flower Composition does not present its flower motifs as copies of nature, neither is it concerned with realistic structure or form. Instead, it transforms and portrays flowers in optical-graphical movement creating a composition which is specially suited to fashion fabrics.

300 pages, 400 motifs, monochrome - black/white
book box, bound in cotton canvas - black.
single plates: *31 x 43 cm,*

NATURAL FLOWER & HERBS

68 suggested variations presenting an immense number of different floral motifs based upon mountain flowers and herbs. The flower plates are painted with an extremely high quality more than 150 years ago by a Japanese artist with a particular handwriting.
The book is reproduced in a monochrome technique. Each composition is printed on a single plate (horizontal 31 x 43 cm). In addition the book contains 8 plates in a polychrome version (full color).
The edition includes a rich album which names all the flowers and herbs by reduced illustrations.

76 plates, 8 full-page color plates, incl. album,
single plates: *31 x 43 cm,*
book box, bound in cotton canvas - blue.

FLORAL ART

60 plates of floral designs of 1932, when the book was published for the first time. Floral Art - Decoration and Design certainly is a work of the kind that all should welcome, whether they are primarily interested in the design of flowers as such or as integral elements of decoration.
The illustrations are as practical as they are varied and abundant and finely reproduced in colorphoto system.
Size of each reproduction: 16 x 23 cm.

60 plates, all in color, **Limited Edition,**
single plates: *31 x 43 cm, book box, bound in cotton canvas - dark red.*

BELVEDERE BOOK BOXES

FLOWER & ORNAMENT

This book is influenced by the "Jugenstil". All motifs were originated between 1910-1920. On 72 plates are presented more than 450 floral & ornamental motifs, printed in a polychrome version - all in full color. There are mainly ideas from or for wallpaper, mural painting, interior design and carpets, mostly in combination: graphic or ornamental elements composed with floral motifs.

72 plates, 450 motifs, all in color, incl. album,
single plates: 31 x 43 cm,
book box, bound in cotton canvas - red.

BLUMEN

72 floral plates (printed in polychrome & monochrome) with many single motifs. The volume is divided into three sections - I. 24 floral plates with 60 different motifs, originated around 1915, all in color. II. 24 floral designs, possible adaptions/interpretations from the originals, also all in color. III. 24 basic compositions with elements from the designs of part II, in monochrome - black and white.
The edition includes an album which indicates all flowers' names are shown in the book.

72 plates, polychrome & monochrome, incl. album, single plates: 31 x 43 cm, book box, bound in cotton canvas - light brown.

THE PLANTS OF 1917

125 floral reproductions - all in full color - showing garden plants of the four seasons. In the yeear 1917, based on European flowers, the plates were painted in Japanese handwriting in watercolor technique with an extremely high quality. The motifs are divided in 50 plates of the spring season, 50 plates of the summer season and 25 plates with both - autumn and winter flowers.
The edition indicates in the front page all flowers names which are shown in the book.

66 plates, 125 colorphoto reproductions, all in color, single plates: 34 x 48 cm, book box, bound in cotton canvas - green.
Limited Edition.

BEAUTIES OF NATURE

The volume shows 48 single plates with beautiful flower illustrations, painted in 1896. The reproduction is made in colorphoto system. Each volume is handmade. The book is represented in a box and includes an album which indicates all flowers name are shown in the book. Beauties of Nature is an individual an limited edition.

48 plates, all in color, incl. album,
Limited Edition, *single plates: 31 x 43 cm, book box, bound in cotton canvas - grey.*

BELVEDERE BOOK BOXES

The book boxes of the Edition Belvedere offer professional material for artists, stylists and designers in the field of textile and fashion. The above mentioned boxes are strictly limited editions and they are available only directly from the publisher. For further information, conditions and prices write to:
EDITION BELVEDERE CO. LTD., 00196 ROME/ITALY, PIAZZALE FLAMINIO 19, TEL. (06) 360.44.88/360.29.60.

All volumes are representing single plates, mostly 31 x 43 cm, on heavy paper, and they are collect in a box, bound in cotton canvas.

BELVEDERE BOOK BOXES

BELVEDERE - PAPERBACKS
VOLUME 4

The traditional Japanese folding books often appear to us as fantastic, richly-colored picture-books. They are characterized by a highly subtle color scheme, and a strongly emotional, graphically oriented composition. Their illustrations convey a story character. The calligraphic energy of the linear style, the powerful effect of the color contrasts, the black-and-white painting and the surface pattern of the composition, all radiate an imaginative, coherent vitality. The immediately decorative tendency is clearly apparent. The almost graphically ordered flower motifs seem to arise from the same motivations which led to the creation of the artfully arranged flower- and stone-gardens. ORIENTAL FLOWERS illustrates such folding books – without doubts part of Japanese decorative painting – on over 200 pages, most of them in color, as well as reproducing patterns from the various arts and crafts, such as porcelain, ceramics, faience, lacquer-work, kimonos or textiles.

ISBN 88-7070-005-4

DECOR

SOMERSET COLLEGES

T0018404

COLLEGE LIBRARY

SOMERSET COLLEGE OF ARTS AND TECHNOLOGY
Wellington Road, Taunton, Somerset TA1 5AX
(283403 ext 236)

Author: ....

Title: ..DECOR..

Class:..745........................ Stock No:.....178752.L...........

This book is due for return on or before the last date shown below.

-9. JUN. 1989	20. NOV
30. JUN. 1989	20. NOV
-6. OCT. 1989	
10. MAY 1991	25. FEB 98
10. JAN 92	12. MAY 98
16. JUN 92	CANCELLED 02 APR
08. JAN 93	
29. SEP	
29. NOV	
07. FEB 94	
07. NOV 94	

DECOR

745   178752 L

£29.00

BELVEDERE